Neymar. Like so many great artists, Brazil's greatest footballer is known by only one name. The only fellow countryman to compare to him for sheer ability is the world's greatest ever player, Pelé. But Neymar has pushed the great man all the way when it comes down to skills, flicks and tricks.

But there has always been more to his game than just the fancy stuff, for Neymar not only promises so much, he also delivers the goods. A teenage child star for his first club Santos and then the Brazil national side, the player known to his family as Neymar Jr or Neymar da Silva Santos Junior – to give him his full name – has won numerous honours.

Although his father was a footballer, Neymar was not born into wealth and, like many before him, honed his skills on the streets. He made his name in São Paulo, with Santos, before becoming a truly global star at Barcelona and Brazil's national side.

Neymar made his professional debut aged just 17. Unprecedented glory for Santos soon followed as he helped the club win two consecutive regional titles, the Copa do Brasil, and the 2011 Copa Libertadores, the Santos's first continental title in almost 50 years.

He was voted South American Footballer of the Year in 2011 and again in 2012. Barcelona could not wait any longer to lure him to Spain and La Liga, where he became an even bigger success.

It was in Europe that he became part of the world-famous M-S-N goalscoring trio with fellow South Americans Luis Suárez and Lionel Messi. They won the treble of La Liga, Copa del Rey and UEFA Champions League in 2015, the year Neymar came third in the FIFA Ballon d'Or awards.

Many great prospects have come out of Brazil since Pelé, but few can match Neymar's feats. Maybe his greatest achievement so far was captaining Brazil to 2016 Olympic Games gold medal glory, at home in Rio, the one major football trophy Brazil had not won.

Neymar scored his 105th and final goal for Barcelona as they won the 2017 Copa del Rey. He also helped Brazil qualify for the 2018 World Cup. All this persuaded French club Paris Saint-Germain to break the world transfer record by triggering his release clause and signing him for €222m in August 2017. He scored on his debut and has continued getting goals since.

Neymar is flanked by Phillippe Coutinho (left) and Gabriel Jesus after scoring for Brazil against Argentina in 2016.

Neymar is all smiles as he faces the media at the Parc des Princes after his world record transfer to Paris Saint-Germain was confirmed.

THE EARLY YEARS

Street football is the starting point for thousands of Brazilians and, for Neymar, it was no different. It was where he honed his skills.

Neymar da Silva Santos Junior was born on 5 February 1992 in the Mogi das Cruzes area of São Paulo to his mother Nadine and his father Neymar da Silva Santos Sr, who had been a footballer himself. It would not be long before the child would inherit his dad's passion for the beautiful game.

However, what came first for the youngster was not the 11-a-side format of the game in which he would go on to become a world famous player.

Like many young Brazilians, Neymar cut his teeth playing on the street with his mates, while he also began to hone his signature ball control while playing Futsal, the five-a-side game played with a smaller ball, where quick feet and even quicker thinking are the key.

Then, when he was already madly in love with the game, two family moves in 2003 shaped the 11-year-old's life forever, as he began to plot his path to superstardom.First they moved the 120km from Mogi das Cruzes to the coastal region of São Vicente, where he joined the youth set-up at Portuguesa Santista.

The club, founded in 1917 in Santos by descendants of the city's Portuguese settlers, competes in the Brazilian lower leagues and has the nickname Briosa, a term which means both courageous and graceful. Appropriately they were two of the superlatives which would have been perfect to describe the young Neymar, who was already beginning to emerge as a star of the future.

His performances at Portuguesa Santista were enough to catch the attention of Santos FC, who were quick to snap him up. So the family were soon on the move again, relocating near to the team's Vila Belmiro home.

Now in the youth set-up at one of Brazil's biggest clubs, Neymar flourished. Following in the footsteps of famous compatriots like Elano and Alex, who also came through the academy with Santos, he was in the perfect place to progress.

However, few would have predicted the impact he would have once he made the step into the club's first team at the tender age of 17.

Neymar developed his skills playing Futsal and it was clear from a young age he would work hard to make it to the top.

Neymar wears the No.7 shirt as he celebrates scoring for his first major club in Brazil, the legendary Santos.

PLAYING FOR SANTOS

After joining Santos in 2003, Neymar took six years to make his senior debut, although the secret was out way before then.

Reports of a teenage prodigy with quicksilver feet and goalscoring ability had already spread to Europe, where Real Madrid, among others, were keeping a close eye on his situation.

Indeed, Neymar even travelled to Madrid when he was just 14 to join the Bernabeu "Galacticos", the side that boasted global stars such as Ronaldo, Zinedine Zidane and David Beckham. However, the deal never materialized and it was at Santos where he made his name.

On 7 March 2009, aged just 17, Neymar pulled on the famous white jersey for the first team, when Santos travelled to Oeste. He had been named as a substitute, and the match was still goalless when he was sent on to replace Mauricio Molina in the 59th minute. His arrival improved matters and Santos went on to secure a 2–1 win, scoring two goals in the final 26 minutes.

He made his full senior debut eight days later when he was selected to start against Mogi Mirim. And he did not disappoint, scoring his first

Neymar shows off his great acrobatic skills that persuaded Santos to make him a first team regular as a teenager.

Santos goal after 72 minutes and helping the side to a 3–0 victory.

He was substituted in the 80th minute to rapturous applause as the Vila Belmiro saluted the official arrival of their latest prodigy, who had so far lived up to the hype which had been the talk of Santos supporters for many months.

But it would be a bittersweet season for Neymar, who finished his debut campaign with 14 goals in 48 appearances, as the team suffered a painful defeat in the final of the 2009 Campeonato Paulista.

The teenager started both games in the two-legged semi-final against Palmeiras, scoring in the first, which helped them to a 4–2 aggregate victory. However, in the final they faced Corinthians, unbeaten in their 19 games that season, fronted by Brazilian icon Ronaldo. And it was the old master who made the difference,

Neymar with the Campeonato Paulista trophy – the "Paulistao" – Brazil's oldest professional league, formed in 1902.

scoring twice in a 3–1 first-leg win. So, when the two sides drew 1–1 in the second leg, Neymar and Santos were forced to settle for the runners-up spot. But he would bounce back in style.

Nothing gives Neymar more pleasure than scoring goals. This one was in a Santos away game in the Paulistao.

Neymar was soon famous worldwide, but he kept his eye on the prize for Santos.

Neymar poses with the trophy he won as player of the year in the 2010 Campeonato Paulista.

After such pain in 2009, Neymar was not about to let it happen to him again as he kicked off his first full season in the Santos senior side.

With peerless close control and a deep bag of tricks, the youngster was the sort of fan-friendly forward Santos had been waiting for. But during a season of many high points, one match stands out above all as a demonstration of the force Neymar had already become.

On 15 April 2010, a little more than one year after making his full debut for the club, Neymar was selected for the visit of Guarani in the Copa do Brasil. It would turn out to be a very long day for the away side's defence.

There were only two minutes on the clock when Neymar struck, tucking home a penalty with aplomb, before doubling his tally in the 29th minute. Strike partner Robinho got in on the act with two goals too, while substitute Marcel also notched, but by the end of the clash Neymar had struck five times in an 8–1 thrashing.

Such goalscoring form would be the cornerstone of Santos' surge to the final of the Campeonato Paulista, as they won 15 of their 19 fixtures before beating São Paulo home and away in the semi-final.

But they needed Neymar in the final to make sure more pain would be avoided after a 3–2 win over Santo André in the first leg threatened to turn into a nightmare in the second.

Less than a minute had gone, when Nunes struck to level the aggregate scoreline for André, but two goals from Neymar ensured they lost only 3–2, securing a 5–5 aggregate draw. This was enough for Santos to claim the trophy. Following that performance, which took his 2010 Paulista goal tally to 14 in 19 games, he was named the best player in the competition.

By now, stories of Santos' teenage magician had spread and newspaper reports claimed English clubs West Ham and Chelsea had made big-money offers to take him to the Premier League. But the Brazilian side resisted – and would be repaid in some style the following season.

Securing the Campeonato in 2010 was one thing, but what Neymar helped Santos do in 2011 etched his name into the club's folklore forever.

Indeed the year was a big one for the striker all round as he was named the South American Footballer of the Year by a record margin, while an incredible solo goal against Flamengo secured him the FIFA Puskás Award.

Santos won the Campeonato for the second consecutive year, with Neymar scoring a respectable four goals in 11 appearances, but it was his performances in that year's Copa Libertadores which proved he had now reached a new level altogether.

The Brazilian club reached the knockout stages of the competition after coming second in Group Five, level on points with first-placed Cerro Poteno of Paraguay, Neymar having scored three goals in their six group games.

He then scored goals in the quarter- and semi-finals too, helping fire Santos to only their fourth Copa Libertadores Final in their history, where they would face Uruguayan powerhouse Peñarol. The two clubs had met in the same fixture back in 1962, with Santos coming out on top – and it was Neymar who ensured that history repeated itself.

After a razor-tight first leg finished 0–0, the 19-year-old finally found a breakthrough 47 minutes into the second match. Danilo doubled the advantage for Santos in the 69th minute

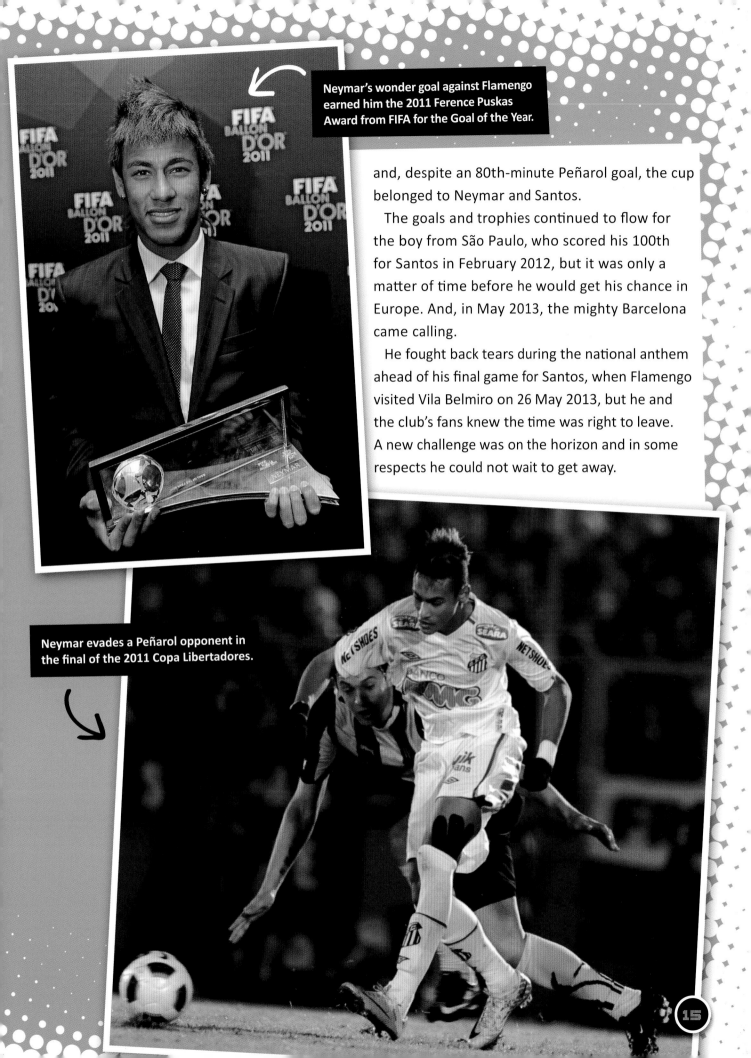

and, despite an 80th-minute Peñarol goal, the cup belonged to Neymar and Santos.

The goals and trophies continued to flow for the boy from São Paulo, who scored his 100th for Santos in February 2012, but it was only a matter of time before he would get his chance in Europe. And, in May 2013, the mighty Barcelona came calling.

He fought back tears during the national anthem ahead of his final game for Santos, when Flamengo visited Vila Belmiro on 26 May 2013, but he and the club's fans knew the time was right to leave. A new challenge was on the horizon and in some respects he could not wait to get away.

Neymar evades a Peñarol opponent in the final of the 2011 Copa Libertadores.

BRAZIL'S HERO

A lot of pressure has been put on Neymar's young shoulders, but it appears he is thriving as an international footballer despite it.

Neymar arrived on the international stage aged 18. Brazil were already the most successful team in the history of the game, having won the World Cup five times and as the only country to have played in every tournament. Yet Neymar's impact on the international stage has eclipsed some of the greatest players his country ever produced.

His international journey began in a friendly against USA, in July 2010, soon after Brazil's World Cup quarter-final loss to the Netherlands. It was apparent Brazil had a new superstar as Neymar took just 28 minutes to score his first goal for his country in a 2–0 victory.

Quickly becoming a key player for Brazil, Neymar was selected to play in the 2012 London Olympics, where they lost to Mexico in the final.

A year later Neymar was assigned the team's famous No.10 shirt, previously worn by Pelé, as Brazil lifted the Confederations Cup. Neymar won the Golden Ball for player of the tournament.

By 2014, he had the weight of a nation on his shoulders as Brazil hosted the World Cup. He was expected to deliver a sixth world crown, but was injured the quarter-final and, without him, Brazil were crushed by Germany in the semi-final. It was a time for change and, during the 2015 Copa América, Neymar was appointed team captain.

He remained captain as Brazil hosted the 2016 Olympic Games, in Rio. The aim was to make amends for the World Cup and heal a nation.

They did not disappoint, winning a tense final in a sudden-death penalty shoot-out against, of all teams, Germany. And no prizes for guessing who took and scored the decisive spot-kick – Neymar!

Neymar resigned as captain after the Olympics, to focus on giving his very best for his country. And he delivered, helping Brazil become the first team to qualify for the 2018 World Cup finals and scoring in the decisive 3–0 victory over Paraguay.

He said: "First of all I want to help my team, always, and then I think about pushing the limits, reaching the marks of games and goals.

"I am very happy for this moment, not only mine, but also my team-mates. We are achieving our goals, which is to win and reach the World Cup as well."

The teenage Neymar sinks to his knees in celebration of his first international goal in a 2010 friendly against USA.

Neymar was Brazil's star attraction when he played for his country at the London 2012 Olympic Games.

Neymar, in the famous No.10 shirt, jumps into Paulinho's arms after a World Cup qualifying win against Argentina.

17

NEYMAR'S GREAT SANTOS GOALS

Neymar hit an incredible 135 goals for his boyhood club Santos, and these are five of his very best strikes ...

SANTOS 10, NAVIRAIENSE 0
Copa do Brasil, 10 March 2010

A match for Naviraiense keeper Aldo to forget as he let in 10 goals, including two from Neymar. The pick of the bunch was his first. Santos were scoring at will, but Neymar's skills set him above the rest as the ball seemed to be glued to his boot when he nipped in and out of three defenders inside the penalty area before rounding the goalkeeper with a final drop of the shoulders to finish with ease.

SANTOS 4, FLAMENGO 5
Brasileiro, 27 July 2011

This was a great solo effort. Neymar's outrageous close control deceived two defenders on the left wing before he cut inside to play a quick one-two. The Brazilian then skilfully nudged the ball beyond a third defender by flicking the ball from boot to boot and then curled his shot beyond the stranded goalkeeper with the outside of his foot.

Santos captain Robinho pretends to polish Neymar's boot after his first Copa do Brasil goal against Naviraiense.

SANTOS 3, KASHIWA REYSOL 1
**FIFA Club World Cup,
14 December 2011**

A beautiful goal that only a few other players in the world could dream of scoring. Neymar received possession of the ball on the edge of the penalty area before feinting inside onto his left foot to leave a defender stranded on the floor. The Santos star then picked his spot before finding the top corner.

Neymar shows his powers of concentration as he curls in a wonder goal in the 2011 FIFA Club World Cup.

SANTOS 3, INTERNACIONAL 1
Copa Libertadores, 7 March 2012

Neymar has the unique ability to run as fast with the ball as he does without it. In this perfect example of that ability, the Brazilian showed tremendous power and strength to hold off defenders before clinically lofting the ball over the advancing goalkeeper.

Neymar tries to encourage the Santos crowd after scoring his great goal against Internacional in the Copa Libertadores.

SANTOS 2, ATLÉTICO MINEIRO 2
Brasileiro, 17 October 2012

Another classic display of Neymar's unrelenting pace and power while in possession. This time he left three defenders trailing behind him before he showed the ice-cool composure that has made him one of the world's best. Poor Atlético keeper Victor had no chance of stopping this one.

SANTOS MILESTONES

JULY 2003
Neymar, 11, officially joins the Youth Academy at Santos. The signing of the young prodigy means he follows in the footsteps of club greats Pepe, Pelé and Robinho.

MARCH 2006
Santos fear they have lost their favourite son when Neymar almost joins Spanish giants Real Madrid following a training camp there shortly after his 14th birthday.

7 MARCH 2009
Neymar makes his debut for Santos at the age of 17, coming on for the last 30 minutes in a 2–1 win against Oeste.

15 MARCH 2009
History is made as Neymar scores his first senior goal for Santos, striking in the 73rd minute against Mogi Mirim. Just a shame that only 16,000 lucky people were there to witness the start of an incredible run of goals.

15 APRIL 2010
Continuing his rise to the top a year later, Neymar scores a remarkable five goals in an 8–1 thrashing of Guarani, in the qualifying stages of the Brazilian Cup. Santos proceed to win the Campeonato Paulista with Neymar scoring 14 goals in 19 games.

9 DECEMBER 2010
Aged just 18, Neymar comes an impressive third in the South American Footballer of the Year vote behind Argentine duo Juan Verón and Andrés D'Alessandro.

27 JULY 2011
A sensational solo goal against Flamengo is not enough to win the match, but it earns him the FIFA Puskás Award, handed to the scorer of the "most beautiful goal of the year".

31 DECEMBER 2011
Neymar wins the South American Footballer of the Year award for the first time and by a record margin.

5 FEBRUARY 2012
On the day of his 20th birthday, Neymar scores his 100th professional goal – against Palmeiras in the Campeonato Paulista.

31 DECEMBER 2012
Neymar retains his South American Footballer of the Year title after a blistering season, including netting 14 goals in the Campeonato Brasileiro. He wins the award ahead of Brazilian fellow countryman Ronaldinho.

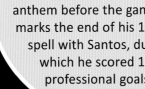

26 MAY 2013
An emotional farewell in his last Santos match – against Flamengo. Neymar cries during the national anthem before the game that marks the end of his 10-year spell with Santos, during which he scored 135 professional goals.

Neymar shows his pride at wearing the Brazil No.10 short, first made world famous by the great Pelé.

WINNING THE CONFEDERATIONS CUP

After the painful and surprising nature of Brazil's defeat in the final at the London 2012 Olympic Games, Neymar was determined not to let the 2013 FIFA Confederations Cup end in the same manner.

The competition pits the winners of the six continental championships against each other, along with the FIFA World Cup holders and hosts, to determine who is the best, and, having won the title in both 2005 and 2009, Brazil were aiming for an unprecedented hat-trick.

As it was taking place on home soil, the forward and his teammates knew it was the perfect opportunity to put things right – and they did so in style.

Extra pressure was piled on to Neymar's shoulders before a ball was kicked as head coach Luiz Felipe Scolari handed him the Brazil No.10 jersey, worn by Pelé and so many legends of Brazilian football. His heir apparent was ready to live up to the huge expectations in front of his own people.

It started well for Neymar, who scored the first goal of the tournament, three minutes into a routine 3–0 defeat of Japan on 15 June 2013.

Spain's Alvaro Arbeloa can only watch on as Neymar's shot gives Iker Casillas no chance of saving his effort in the final.

Neymar shows what winning the trophy means as he kisses the Confederations Cup.

Another goal, and an assist, followed in Brazil's second Group A game as they beat Mexico 2–0, and then Neymar scored a fine free-kick in their 4–2 win against Italy in their final game which confirmed them as group winners.

A dramatic 2–1 semi-final win over Uruguay, secured with an 86th-minute goal, was enough to book their place in the final, where Neymar once again took centre stage.

On 30 June 2013 Brazil faced the might of reigning world and European champions Spain at the iconic Maracaná Stadium. On his country's biggest stage, Neymar, still only 21, turned in arguably the best international performance so far in his career to inspire his country to a crushing 3–0 victory.

His goal in the 44th minute came in between a double for strike partner Fred and secured Brazil's famous hat-trick of Confederations Cup victories His display that day, with the No.10 on his back, was enough to earn him the Golden Ball, awarded to the tournament's outstanding player.

Nobody across any of FIFA's six confederations could have any argument.

AT HOME WITH NEYMAR

There are few things that Neymar loves more than football, but at the very top of that list is his son David Lucca da Silva Santos.

The baby was born on 24 August 2011 at the São Luiz hospital in his father's home state of Sáo Paulo, and Neymar has doted on the boy ever since.

Family is a cornerstone of Neymar's life and he enjoys a strong relationship with his sister Rafaella Beckran. They both have tattoos in each other's honour – in fact, the striker has two!

Just as he did in Brazil, where he lived very close to the Santos ground, Neymar lived in a luxury three-storey property near the Camp Nou in Barcelona. And, on moving to Paris, his home was close to PSG's training ground. Back in his native Brazil, he has a place in the Jardim Acapulco, on Pernambuco's beach, in Guarujá, São Paulo.

When it comes to a holiday, Neymar owns places along the coast of Brazil's Santa Catarina, where he likes to go wakeboarding.

A keen cards player whose favourite game is poker, he also plays the piano. He enjoys being at home watching TV – he is a *Games of Thrones* fan,

Neymar sits proudly with a potential Brazil football superstar of the future – his son David.

but also likes *Prison Break* – and he loves to play video games on his Playstation. And not many weeks pass without a new Neymar hairstyle.

The devout Christian is passionate about charity work, donates up to 10 per cent of his earnings to his church and stages regular charity matches with his close friend and fellow Brazilian player Nené.

Neymar is fanatical about music and a video of him dancing to Michel Telo's hit "Ai Se Eu Te Pego" went viral. He later appeared on stage at one of the pop star's concerts and incorporated the moves into one of his renowned goal celebrations.

Music has been around him since a young age. He once recalled: "I have an aunt and uncle who play the guitar, so there has always been music at home. Samba, pagoda, gospel and other rhythms. And I've always liked dancing."

In 2013, he became the first Brazilian to grace the front cover of *Time* magazine, beneath the headline "The Next Pelé", completing his transformation to genuine household name.

Celebrating the UEFA Champions League victory, Neymar displays one of two tattoos he has of his sister Rafaella Beckran.

From one Santos and Brazil legend to another, the great Pelé shows affection for his successor for club and country.

NEYMAR'S SUPER SKILLS

Neymar's amazing array of tricks and awesome talents are what make him one of the world's greatest players.

TERRIFIC TECHNIQUE

Once Neymar has beaten a defender, he retains his composure and often dispatches tremendous curling shots beyond goalkeepers. The Brazilian is able to use either foot to guide the ball wherever he wants it to go. His technical ability, combined with a cool head under pressure, is what makes him so prolific in front of goal.

DEADLY DELIVERY

As well as his goalscoring prowess, Neymar is often the architect of goals scored by his team-mates. The Paris Satin-Germain star has the ability to beat defenders and whip dangerous crosses in, aimed at his strikers. His assists in a season are often in double figures, making him an all-round world-class player.

DAZZLING DRIBBLING

Speed alone is not enough to make a world-class player. It is Neymar's incredible dribbling at full speed which sets him apart from other top players. He bamboozles defenders with his unbelievable balance and ability to keep the ball just inches away from his feet.

THE CHOP

One of the most outrageous tricks in his box, Neymar's "chop" gives defenders sleepless nights. First he draws the defender towards him, then suddenly changes direction, flicking the ball with the opposite foot to gain an extra yard on the defender. On numerous occasions Neymar has displayed this trick and beaten goalkeepers from all angles.

Neymar, wearing a Paris Saint-Germain hat, shows off his skills in training with his new French club.

BALL CONTROL

Neymar's game is about pace and his dribbling ability. His ball control is matched only by ex-Barcelona team-mate Lionel Messi. Neymar has a rare gift of being as fast in possession as he is without the ball. Few players have the ability to draw several defenders towards him, and so open up space elsewhere on the pitch.

PARTY TRICKS

To really rub salt into the wounds, Neymar not only has the ability to bully defenders into making mistakes but he can also wind them up with his outrageous flicks and tricks. Not only standing still, the Brazilian can throw defenders off guard with step-overs and dazzling feet while at full pelt. His playing style makes him one of the most exciting players to watch.

Neymar has such great close control it often takes more than one opponent to try and stop him in his tracks.

27

NEYMAR'S GREAT BARÇA GOALS

The Brazilian has been deadly in front of goal since he signed for Barcelona in 2013, and here are five of his most spectacular efforts for the Spanish giants ...

BARCELONA 6, RAYO VALLECANO 0
La Liga, 15 February 2014

The Brazilian receives a pass from Andrés Iniesta on the halfway line and decides the four defenders in front of him are no barrier to scoring. He glides his way through them all to complete a 6–0 win with a thunderous strike from 25 yards. One of his best.

Neymar in trademark celebration mode as he marks a Barcelona goal against Elche in the Copa del Rey.

REAL MADRID 3, BARCELONA 1
La Liga, 25 October 2014

Luis Suárez, on his debut, finds Neymar on the right-hand side of the Madrid area. Neymar cuts inside, runs along the edge of the box, baffles the defenders facing him, and finally leaves goalkeeper Iker Casillas flat-footed with the sweetest of low right-foot shots.

BARCELONA 5, ELCHE 0
Copa del Rey, 8 January 2015

Neymar controls a Lionel Messi pass with his chest before stepping towards the penalty area, going past a bemused defender, and setting his sights on goal. He unleashes a tremendous strike which arrows into the top corner of the net, to seal a convincing victory for Barcelona.

SEVILLA 2, BARCELONA 2
La Liga, 11 April 2015

A classic example of the perfect free-kick. Neymar fires the ball with his right foot from just outside the area, displaying remarkable ability to lift it up over a jumping Sevilla defensive wall with enough topspin to bring the ball dipping down into the top left-hand corner. Keeper Rico González took one look at the ball and did not bother to move. No point when Neymar strikes a ball like this.

BARCELONA 3, PARIS ST GERMAIN 1
Champions League, 10 December 2015

This crucial and spectacular 25-yard strike ensured that Barcelona would end up as winners of Group F. Neymar started with the ball on the edge of the centre circle, from where he ran directly at goal and let fly from distance. The goalkeeper had no chance.

BARCELONA 3, VILLARREAL 0
La Liga, 8 November 2015

A wonderful individual goal. Neymar loses the defender by brilliantly lobbing the ball over his head before volleying clinically beyond the goalkeeper.

Neymar scored a wonder goal against Villarreal in La Liga, and this series of photos shows his control, skill and finishing power.

TRAINING WITH NEYMAR

The Paris Saint-Germain star may be blessed with incredible natural talent, but he also knows that will count for nothing unless he continues to work hard on the training ground.

He started out playing with his father, a former professional, who taught him the basics and a great work ethic. He trained on many of his close skills in street matches and then by playing Futsal before graduating to the full-size game.

Neymar believes that, however good a player is, there is always room for improvement. He said, when discussing training: "You always have to improve. From when I was little, my father told me to finish a training session exhausted, and that is what I do to this day."

Before Neymar's move to European football in 2013, there were question marks over his physical capabilities and whether he would be able to adapt to a different style of football.

When Luis Enrique became Barcelona boss in 2014 he was influential in helping Neymar turn into the physical powerhouse he is now.

He spent hours refining his physical attributes, and the incredible results prove just how seriously he has taken his training.

Neymar trains with a smile on his face under the watchful eye of Barcelona coach Luis Enrique.

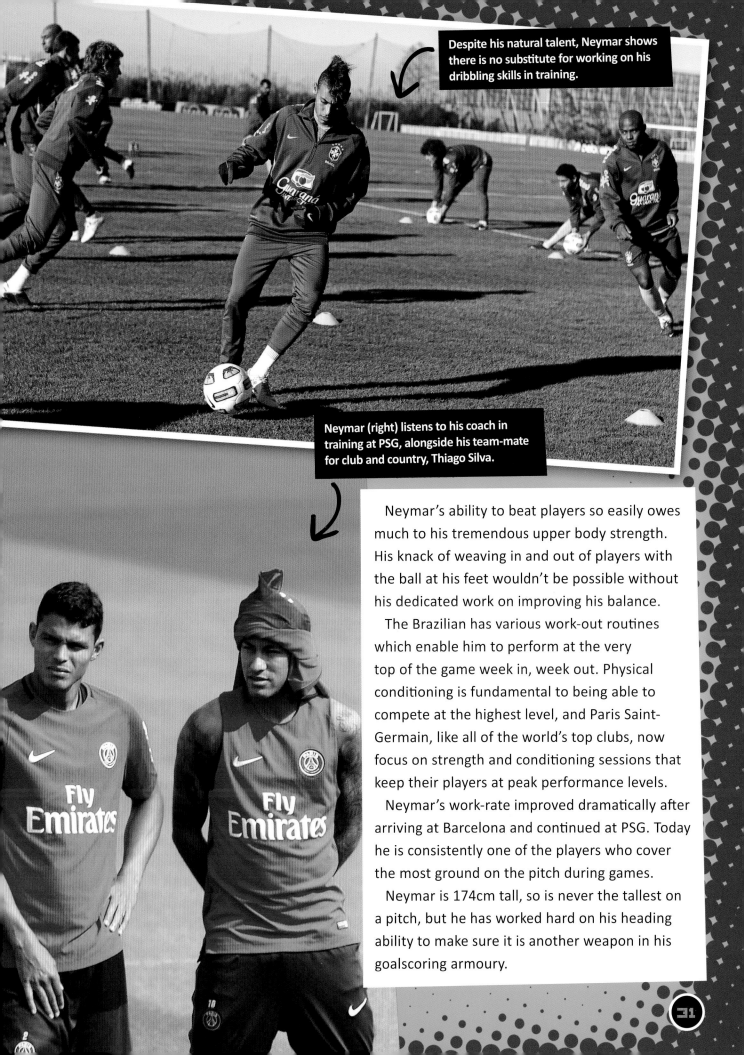

Despite his natural talent, Neymar shows there is no substitute for working on his dribbling skills in training.

Neymar (right) listens to his coach in training at PSG, alongside his team-mate for club and country, Thiago Silva.

Neymar's ability to beat players so easily owes much to his tremendous upper body strength. His knack of weaving in and out of players with the ball at his feet wouldn't be possible without his dedicated work on improving his balance.

The Brazilian has various work-out routines which enable him to perform at the very top of the game week in, week out. Physical conditioning is fundamental to being able to compete at the highest level, and Paris Saint-Germain, like all of the world's top clubs, now focus on strength and conditioning sessions that keep their players at peak performance levels.

Neymar's work-rate improved dramatically after arriving at Barcelona and continued at PSG. Today he is consistently one of the players who cover the most ground on the pitch during games.

Neymar is 174cm tall, so is never the tallest on a pitch, but he has worked hard on his heading ability to make sure it is another weapon in his goalscoring armoury.

BRAZIL MILESTONES

OCTOBER 2009
Neymar first broke onto the international scene during the 2009 Under-17 World Cup. The then teenager scored in the opening game of the tournament against Japan, prompting calls from former greats Pelé and Romário for him to be in the senior squad.

AUGUST 2010
Neymar made his debut for the Brazil senior side at the age of 18 on 10 August 2010 in a friendly against the United States, scoring after 28 minutes in a 2–0 win.

AUGUST 2011
Although now starting for the senior side, Neymar helped Brazil's Under-20s win the 2011 South American U-20 Championship, scoring nine goals during the tournament. The next best tally by any other player was only four.

SEPTEMBER 2012
Neymar scored his first international hat-trick for Brazil on 10 September 2012 during an 8–0 victory over China in Recife.

JUNE 2013
Neymar shone for Brazil during the 2013 Confederations Cup as they went all the way and were crowned champions. The forward scored four goals during the competition and received the Golden Ball for player of the tournament.

JULY 2014
Neymar collected the Bronze Boot at the 2014 World Cup after finishing the tournament with four goals.

OCTOBER 2014
On 14 October 2014, Neymar managed to strike four times for the first time in an international match as he scored all of Brazil's goals in a 4–0 win over Japan in Singapore.

NOVEMBER 2014
Neymar netted 15 goals for Brazil in 2014, ending with two against Turkey on 12 November – and averaging more than a goal a game.

JULY 2014
Neymar was shortlisted for the 2014 World Cup Golden Ball and, after narrowly missing out, was named in the team of the tournament.

OCTOBER 2014
By the age of 22, Neymar had already scored 40 goals in just 50 international matches, making him the fifth highest goalscorer in Brazil's history.

JUNE 2016
Neymar was made captain of Brazil when he was just 22, becoming one of the youngest players to ever hold the role for the country.

AUGUST 2016
Neymar became the first Brazilian to captain the country to a gold medal during the 2016 Rio Olympic Games. Brazil won the final against Germany on penalties at the Maracanã, with Neymar scoring the decisive kick.

MARCH 2017
Neymar again played a pivotal role in Brazil's qualification campaign for the 2018 World Cup in Russia. He scored six goals as the team topped the South America qualifying group, losing only one game.

NEYMAR IN NUMBERS

Football is driven by statistics and, in Neymar's case, some of the numbers are jaw-dropping. Here are a few of them.

'10 This number of goals ensured the forward finished joint top scorer in the Champions League during the 2014–15 season. The Brazilian managed to find the net 10 times, a total matched by Cristiano Ronaldo and Lionel Messi.

37.9 The amazing number, in millions, of fans who follow Neymar on Twitter as of February 2018.

'136 The total number of goals scored by the forward during his time with Santos. Neymar proved to be a formidable force for the Brazilian club, his best season coming in 2012, when he scored 43 times in just 47 games.

9 The number of goals he scored as Brazil won the South American U-20 Championship in 2011. The next best tally was four.

'17 Neymar's age when he made his debut for Santos, in March 2009. The youngster was brought on for the last 30 minutes in a 2–1 win against Oeste. The following week he started and scored his first goal against Mogi Mirim.

60,830,332 The number of Facebook "likes" Neymar has received on his official account as of February 2018.

85
The number of goals Neymar scored for Barcelona in his first three full seasons at the club, 2013–14 to 2015–16.

131
The incredible number of goals scored by Lionel Messi, Luis Suárez and Neymar during the 2015–16 season for the trio known as MSN. The rest of the Barcelona team scored 46 goals.

10,000
The number of shirts, with Neymar's name and number on it, sold on the Brazilian's first day at Paris Saint-Germain.

222
The amount, in millions of euros, that Paris Saint-Germain paid to Barcelona to trigger Neymar's release clause io set in motion his transfer in August 2017.

NEYMAR'S SUPERSTAR TEAMMATES

Neymar has played alongside some of the greatest ever footballers in his time at Barcelona and Paris Saint-Germain.

ANDRÉS INIESTA

The heartbeat of the Barcelona team, the midfielder is the man who makes them tick. Like others at the Nou Camp, Iniesta came through the club's famous La Masia academy before cementing his place in the first team. From an early age the Spaniard had been tipped for a bright future, and shortly after he arrived at Barcelona, aged 12, then-captain Pep Guardiola famously told fellow midfielder Xavi: "You're going to retire me. This lad [Iniesta] is going to retire us all."

EDINSON CAVANI

Since joining Paris Saint-Germain from Napoli in 2013, Cavani has established himself as one of the most lethal finishers in the world. Blessed with strength and speed, the Uruguayan strike partner of Neymar's former Barcelona team-mate Luis Suárez has already scored more than 150 goals for the French club. Incredibly, 49 of those came during the 2016–17 season.

LUIS SUÁREZ

Playing alongside Lionel Messi and Neymar, Suárez was the final piece which completed one of the most lethal forward lines in the history of football. Signed from Liverpool for £65 million in July 2014, Suárez has continued to develop his reputation as one of the most deadly finishers in the world. After scoring 25 goals in his first season, the Uruguayan netted an amazing 59 times during the 2015–16 campaign in just 53 games. Those goals led to Suárez winning the European Golden Shoe for the second time in his career.

LIONEL MESSI

He is undoubtedly one of the greatest players of all time, and defenders have been trying and failing for years to keep the Argentinian quiet. Blessed with lightning quick feet and a lethal left foot, the forward regularly bags more than 40 goals in a season and during the 2011–12 campaign he took that tally to a record-breaking 73. Neymar's arrival at Barcelona has spurred Messi on to new heights, and they formed a trio with Luis Suárez that scored 131 goals over the course of the 2015–16 season.

NEYMAR AND THE NEYMARZETES

Not many footballers have a fan base with their own group name. Well, meet the Neymarzetes, Neymar's troop of most loyal supporters.

Anyone wondering quite how big Neymar's fan base is need only look back at his unveiling at the Nou Camp in June 2013. Some 56,500 Barcelona supporters flocked to the stadium, all so they could catch a glimpse of the club's latest superstar signing. Shown a few tricks and a flash of his big grin, the fans were in love, and the Brazilian's star has only grown since then.

Back in his homeland of Brazil, the forward is worshipped across the country. During the 2014 World Cup, Neymar mania swept across the nation. Billboards, posters and television adverts were dominated by Neymar as he took the tournament by storm. Some fans were even spotted strolling down the Copacabana beach with a cardboard cut-out of their hero!

Across the world people were beginning to realize just how adored Brazil's linchpin was and their eyes were opened to the

Neymar signs a shirt for one of his adoring fans, a massive group made up of men and women, boys and girls.

Neymarzetes. These are the Neymar fans, whose love for the star striker has led to them being given their own name. They adore him in a manner that no other footballer can rival. Whether copying Neymar's latest outrageous hairstyle, or flocking to whatever venue he is due to visit next, the Neymarzetes are one of the most loyal fan groups on the planet.

They have followed Neymar onto social media too. As of February 2018 more than 60 million had liked his official Facebook. Twitter too has fallen under the Brazilian's spell, with almost 38 million following the forward's account. Here, the fans' devotion can be seen and a quick search of #Neymarzetes will give you a glimpse into what Neymar mania has grown into.

Nor does it show any sign of stopping, with Neymar's fan base only increasing as the years go by. Knowing no bounds, the forward has moved into the world of music by releasing his first single "Yo Necesito" (I Need) in September 2016 under the name Neymusico. Supporters of the Brazilian certainly seemed to like what they heard, as a teaser of the track posted on Neymar's Facebook page earned 14 million views and more than 400,000 likes. Chart toppers, beware!

Neymar celebrates Olympic gold medal success by taking a selfie with his happy Brazilian countrymen in Rio.

parades his new Barcelona shirt at the press conference to announce his signing.

PLAYING FOR BARCELONA

Santos is considered Brazil's most famous club. Barcelona is among the world's biggest, so this was a step up for Neymar.

It was on 3 June 2013 that Neymar was officially unveiled as a Barcelona player and the arrival of such a global superstar naturally grabbed everyone's attention. The Nou Camp was filled with 56,500 fans all hoping to catch a glimpse of their new hero.

From the age of 17 to 21, Neymar had played in his native Brazil. But he was expected to need time to adapt to Spanish football. Not so. In a pre-season game against a Thailand XI, he gave a taste of what to expect by scoring in a 7–1 win.

A few weeks later, Neymar made his official debut for the club, coming on as a substitute for Alexis Sanchez as Barcelona once again put seven past their opponents. This time, Levante were the unfortunate side on wrong end of a 7–0 hammering in Barcelona's opening game of the 2013–14 La Liga season.

With the season only a few days old, there was already silverware up for grabs as Barcelona took on Atletico Madrid in the two-legged Spanish Super Cup.

The first leg, at the Vicente Calderon, proved to be a tight affair between two evenly matched teams but, when Atletico took the lead through David Villa, Neymar hit back with his first goal for his new club.

The Brazilian headed home at the back post from Dani Alves to score what turned out to be the winning goal, as Barcelona won the Spanish Super Cup on away goals following a 0–0 draw in the second leg at home.

That, however, turned out to be the only trophy that ended up in the Barcelona trophy cabinet that season. The club was beaten into second place in La Liga by Atletico Madrid.

Neymar was slowly settling into life in Spain, and his tally of 15 goals for the season was an indication of what was to come. He had been particularly impressive in the Champions League during his debut campaign, finding the net four times as Barcelona made the quarter-finals.

Clearly the forward was a fan of Europe's premier club competition and, with Luis Suárez heading to the Nou Camp, Neymar had the trophy in his sights for next season.

Neymar quickly adapted to La Liga's close marking after joining Barcelona.

Neymar [right, with compatriot Dani Alves] gets his hands on his first trophy for Barcelona, the Spanish Super Cup.

After an impressive 2014 World Cup, in which he had been named in the team of the tournament, and the injury which prematurely ended it for him, Neymar returned to Barcelona ready to take Spain by storm in his second season.

The Brazilian and Lionel Messi were joined up front in the autumn by Luis Suárez, who had arrived from Liverpool for £65 million. The trio would go on to form one of the most lethal forward lines in the history of football, scoring 122 goals over the course of the campaign.

Neymar soon thrived as part of the new attack and his hat-trick against Granada in September – before Suárez's debut – saw the Brazilian go on a run of scoring in each of his next five games.

After a season of settling in, fans were beginning to witness Neymar at his best, and by January he had already scored 20 goals. He had managed 15 in all of the previous campaign.

As the season ticked into the final months, the big games came quickly as Barcelona remained on course to secure the treble of La Liga, Copa del Rey and Champions League. However, Neymar was proving up to the task.

The Brazilian notched an impressive 22 La Liga goals as Barcelona pipped Real Madrid to the title and then turned their attention to the next two trophies.

Neymar had been setting the other competitions alight and he scored the second goal as Barça defeated Athletic Bilbao 3–1 in the Copa del Rey final. The strike was Neymar's seventh in the team's run to victory, making him the tournament's joint top scorer.

Now all that was needed to complete a famous treble was a win in the Champions League final over Juventus in Berlin. Neymar rose to the occasion once more, scoring and helping Luis Enrique's side to a 3–1 victory. It was his 10th goal in the competition and he finished joint top scorer in yet another tournament.

Neymar's second season had been a huge success. He ended it with 39 goals and three winner's medals. The boy from Brazil had found a new home.

Neymar holds aloft the impressive La Liga trophy as Barcelona fans celebrate being the best team in Spain.

Neymar and Dani Alves celebrate with the
Copa del Rey trophy after beating Sevilla.

Club trophies do not get
better than the UEFA
Champions League,
which Neymar got his
hands on after Barcelona
beat Juventus in Berlin.

After a stunning second season at the Nou Camp, the pressure was on Neymar to succeed again as Barcelona looked to defend their treble. However, he was forced to miss the start of the season after suffering from the viral infection mumps. It meant he was absent as Barcelona defeated Sevilla to win the UEFA Super Cup for the fifth time in the club's history.

But, once fully fit again, Neymar was soon back in the swing of things as he set about terrorizing opposition defences. By October the Brazilian was back to his best, and his four goals in a 5–2 league win over Rayo Vallecano reminded everyone of his importance to Barcelona.

r (and son) with his teammates, eir children, as they celebrate g the La Liga trophy in 2016.

CAMPI NS

LLIGA 15-16

S'HA DE

Neymar shows great poise and perfect technique as he shoots past Sevilla's Sergio Rico to score in the 2016 Copa del Rey final.

Neymar's form was gaining international recognition too, and he celebrated the start of 2016 by coming third in the voting for the 2015 FIFA Ballon d'Or, World Footballer of the Year, behind his teammate Lionel Messi and Real Madrid's Cristiano Ronaldo.

Now officially the third best player in the world, Neymar grew in confidence as the business end of the season drew closer. However, part of Barcelona's pursuit of their treble ended in April as they were knocked out of the Champions League at the semi-final stage by Atletico Madrid.

The league and cup double was still in their sights, though, and with the help of Neymar's goals the side began to click. Alongside Messi and Luis Suárez, the Brazilian was forming a lethal front three which would go on to score 131 goals by the end of the season.

Neymar chipped in with 31 of those, but undoubtedly his most important one came in the final of the Copa Del Rey. With the league title already secured, Barcelona faced Sevilla in Madrid hoping to secure a second successive domestic double.

The match proved to be tight, and it was still goalless after 90 minutes. Neymar, who had scored in the previous year's final, came to the rescue and sealed victory with near enough the final kick of the game after Jordi Alba had opened the scoring in the first half of extra time.

PLAYING FOR PSG

If ever there was a club made for the dazzling talents of Neymar it was French heavyweights Paris Saint-Germain.

However, for a while, it looked like it might become the transfer that didn't happen.

PSG tried to sign Neymar in the summer of 2016 but could not to prise him away from Barcelona. Instead, a few months later, the Brazilian signed a new five-year deal at Barça which appeared to rule out any chances of a move.

But included in this new contract was a clause which said that a club could sign him only if they stumped up the staggering figure of €222m.

However, although PSG had moved onto alternative transfer targets, the feeling among the club's hierarchy was that there was only one man who could make the impact that they were hoping for.

And so, on 3 August 2017, and after weeks of negotiations, the French capital club decided to pay Neymar's astronomical release clause, in full, to secure the biggest transfer in history.

It meant football fans the world over would be treated to the mouth-watering prospect of Neymar linking up with Kylian Mbappé, who would join the club two weeks later, and Edinson Cavani in a forward line fit to rival even Barcelona's fabled "M-S-N" triumvirate.

By way of a welcome, Javier Pastore even agreed to vacate the famous No. 10 jersey in order for Neymar to claim his favourite number. However, he had to wait for his first chance to wear it due to a late contract wrangle.

It meant he watched PSG's opening game of the 2017–18 season from the stands as Cavani and Pastore scored in a 2-0 win over Amiens – but only after an on-pitch presentation for the €222m man.

Neymar finally made his Ligue 1 bow eight days later in the inauspicious surroundings of Guingamp's Stade de Roudourou, where he punctuated the perfect debut by scoring PSG's final goal in an impressive 3-0 away win.

A week later, his home debut brought another two goals as Neymar kicked off his Parisian story in style. In fact, there would be no stopping him as he scored 19 goals in the 21 games before the end of 2017. It was beginning to look like the boy from Brazil was worth every penny.

Neymar is mobbed by his new Paris Saint-Germain team-mates after

The Brazilian offers a prayer of thanks as he celebrated his first home game for PSG with two goals in a 6–2 win over Toulouse.

NEYMAR AT THE 2014 WORLD CUP

The world will never know what would have happened if Neymar had not suffered that terrible quarter-final injury ...

So fierce was the clamour for Neymar to be included in Brazil's 2010 World Cup squad that more than 14,000 people signed a petition calling for his selection.

However, the Brazil coach Dunga decided against bowing to public pressure and left the young star out. The nation were dumped out by Holland in the quarter-finals and Dunga lost his job shortly afterwards.

Neymar therefore had to wait until 2014 for his first taste of World Cup football but, as at the Confederations Cup a year earlier, he did so on home soil.

By now he was truly his country's poster boy and he revelled in the spotlight, scoring four goals in Brazil's three Group A matches and sending them through to the round of 16 in style.

In the second round, they were taken the distance by South American rivals Chile at the Estádio Mineirão, Belo Horizonte. After drawing 1–1 after extra time, the clash went to penalties and, with the scores locked at 2–2 after four kicks each, it was left to Neymar to book Brazil's quarter-final spot when he kept his cool to score from 12 yards.

But it was in the last eight that disaster struck for Brazil's superstar. Having teed up their opening goal against Colombia, Neymar and his countrymen seemingly were on their way to the semi-final as they led Colombia 2–1 with just two minutes to play.

However, Colombia defender Juan Zúñiga appeared to knee Neymar in the back, and he was substituted straight away. Checks at the hospital confirmed the worst: a fractured

Neymar is congratulated by Brazil substitute Hernanes after scoring his second goal in the 3–1 defeat of Croatia in the opening game.

Neymar sends Chile goalkeeper Claudio Bravo the wrong way with the winning penalty against Chile.

Brazil teammate Marcelo calls for help as Neymar lies in agony, his World Cup over, after a challenge by Colombia's Zúñiga.

vertebra meant that his World Cup adventure was over.

His teammates rallied round and midfielder Fernandinho spoke for them all: "It's a big loss for us. We need to find a way to stay together and become stronger after losing our greatest player. We will try to win this World Cup and for sure we will dedicate it to Neymar."

However, it was not to be. In the semi-final against Germany, without their talisman, Brazil suffered one of the most painful defeats in their history. After conceding five goals in the first 29 minutes, Brazil eventually lost 7–1, their quest for the trophy brought to a stunning end.

NEYMAR AND HIS COACHES

However great Neymar is, without the guidance from his coaches, he could not have achieved much of his glory.

VÁGNER MANCINI

The man who famously gave the 17-year-old Neymar his debut at Santos knew right away this boy was special. However, Mancini took charge of the club during a transitional phase and, just months after giving Neymar the nod in March 2009, he left the club to be replaced by Wanderley Luxemburgo, who himself would leave five months later.

"NEYMAR IS A BEAUTIFUL PLAYER, HE'S DIFFERENT AND WE'RE AWARE OF THIS. HE HAS BEEN ABLE TO TIP THE GAME IN OUR FAVOUR IN THESE LAST MATCHES. HE IS A YOUNGSTER, HE WILL OF COURSE MAKE MISTAKES, BUT WE ARE GOING TO BE VERY PATIENT WITH HIM."
VÁGNER MANCINI

MURICY RAMALHO

After years of regular management changes at Santos, it was Ramalho who steadied the ship in 2011, winning back-to-back Campeonato Paulista titles as well as the Copa Libertadores and the 2012 Recopa Sudamericana. His success was built around Neymar's talent and he left the club during the same summer that the striker headed to Barcelona.

"IT IS MY BELIEF THAT ONE DAY HE'LL BE REGARDED AS THE BEST PLAYER IN THE WORLD. HE'S BEING PATIENT. HE'S GETTING HIMSELF READY AND THERE'S A WHOLE STRUCTURE BEHIND HIM TO ENSURE THAT HE BECOMES THE FUTURE LEADER OF FC BARCELONA."
MURICY RAMALHO

"NEYMAR DOMINATES EVERY FACET OF THE GAME AND KEEPS STRIVING TO IMPROVE. IN TWO MONTHS, HE HAS INTEGRATED INTO OUR SYSTEM. IT IS VERY DIFFICULT TO FIND SUCH PLAYERS OF HIS AGE."

GERARDO MARTINO

GERARDO MARTINO

Soon after Neymar's arrival at Barcelona in 2013, the club appointed Martino as their new manager. It was the Argentinian who handed him his Barça debut, when the new signing came off the bench in a 7–0 rout that was pleasing for the new boss. Martino would become the first Barça manager not to lose any of his first 16 games in charge, but left after just one season having won only the Spanish Super Cup.

UNAI EMERY

After impressive spells in charge at the likes of Valencia and Sevilla in his homeland of Spain, Unai Emery was handed the top job at Paris Saint-Germain in June 2016. A year later, the club delivered him the most expensive player in football history and one of the sport's most bewitching talents in Neymar.

"HE'S EXTRAORDINARY. HE MAKES EVERYONE BENEFIT FROM HIS TALENT. WHEN NEYMAR PROVIDES SOLUTIONS ON THE PITCH, IT IS GOOD FOR THE TEAM AND ALL THOSE WHO LOVE FOOTBALL."

UNAI EMERY

MANO MENEZES

Full name Luiz Antônio Venker de Menezes, "Mano" was the Brazil head coach who first gave Neymar his chance in the national team. However, his tenure in charge of the Seleção was underwhelming and he was sacked in November 2012 after just two years in charge following an early exit in the Copa America and defeat in the gold medal final at the London Olympics.

"I THINK PLAYING IN THE PREMIER LEAGUE COULD ONLY BE GOOD FOR NEYMAR AS IT WOULD BE CONFIRMATION OF HIS DEVELOPMENT. ENGLISH FOOTBALL WOULD MAKE HIM STRONGER AND HELP HIM TO ESCAPE STRONG MARKING. I DON'T SEE ANY PROBLEM."

MANO MENEZES

NEYMAR'S GREAT BRAZIL GOALS

Technique and talent go together when one thinks of Neymar and they have led to some amazing Brazilian goals.

Watched closely by English referee Howard Webb, Neymar prepares to unleash a left-foot volley to score a brilliant opening goal in the 2–0 win over Mexico.

BRAZIL 3, JAPAN 0
Confederations Cup, 15 June 2013

Neymar's spectacular third-minute goal sets hosts Brazil on their way to a comfortable victory over Japan in the opening game of the Confederations Cup. The striker, unveiled as a Barcelona player 12 days earlier, connects with Fred's knockdown on the edge of the area and sends a blistering shot into the top corner.

BRAZIL 2, MEXICO 0
Confederations Cup, 19 June 2013

A crucial and spectacular 25-yard strike to leave Brazil certain to qualify for the semi-finals from Group A. Neymar received the b on the edge of the centre circle, ran toward the goal and let fly from distance, giving Jos Corona no chance of making a save.

ITALY 2, BRAZIL 4
Confederations Cup, 23 June 2013

Neymar is already the star of this tournament before scoring with a wonder free-kick. Fouled 25 yards out, he has the opportunity to shoot, but with the best keeper in the world to beat. However, Gianluigi Buffon is left rooted to the spot as Neymar's shot curls into the top corner. It is his 23rd goal in 37 internationals.

CAMEROON 1, BRAZIL 4
World Cup, 23 June 2014

Neymar scores twice in a great display as Brazil reach the World Cup knockout stage. His second goal shows the full range of his ability. Running towards the box, Neymar cuts onto his right foot, wrong-foots two defenders and beats Cameroon's keeper with a crisp low shot against the direction in which he is running.

There are few better free-kick experts in the world, as Neymar shows with this curling effort against Italy, in 2013.

BRAZIL 1, GERMANY 1 (BRAZIL WIN 5–4 ON PENS)
Olympic Games gold medal match, 21 August 2016

Brazil's fans had been waiting forever to celebrate winning the men's football gold medal at the Olympic Games. After losing in the London 2012 final, Neymar won it in the Rio 2016 gold medal game. In the penalty shoot-out, he nervelessly sent German goalkeeper Timo Horn the wrong way with the last kick.

Neymar wins Olympic gold by sending German keeper Timo Horn the wrong way from the penalty spot to win the shoot-out for Brazil.

GLOBAL SUPERSTAR

As one of the superstars of the biggest sport on the planet, it is no surprise that Neymar is known all over the world. Everywhere he goes people are desperate to catch a glimpse of the Brazilian, even if it is only for a moment.

"I cannot go anywhere without being recognized," said Neymar in 2013. "People even recognize me in New York. Strange things do happen. A guy once asked me if he could have my shirt. It wasn't even a Santos shirt. It was just a regular shirt."

Given his talent and style, Neymar is gold dust to advertising companies and some of the world's biggest brands have snapped him up. He is one of Nike's marquee names and he is often seen marketing the latest boots. Many other multi-national corporations have signed up the Brazilian to be the face of their products.

It was estimated that Neymar's annual salary was around €30 million with another €22 million in advertising deals, ranking him second on the list of footballer earnings in Europe in 2017. Only ex team-mate Lionel Messi is ahead of him.

Neymar's face does not just adorn television adverts and billboards, but also magazines and newspapers. After becoming the first Brazilian athlete to be on the front of *Time* magazine in February 2013, he has become one of the most googled and read-about footballers on the planet.

Nike have created a special Neymar football boot, based on the same brand concept as Michael Jordan's legendary basketball sneakers.

54

His global reach has expanded into the world of social media, and Neymar is now established as one of the most followed athletes. Almost 100 million people from all corners of the globe follow him on Facebook and Twitter combined, making his every move a news story.

Neymar's feats have been immortalized by a waxwork of him created by Madame Tussauds, now on display in Orlando, Florida, USA. "I'm looking at my twin brother," he remarked upon coming face to face with the figure of him in celebration.

Just when you thought Neymar's star could not get any bigger, it did just that in August 2017 when he left Barcelona for Paris Saint-Germain. The French club paid a world record €222m (£200m) to sign the forward, making him the most expensive player in the history of the game.

The world's media surround Neymar as they try to get a picture of the star and his Olympic gold medal.

Neymar and Paris Saint-Germain president Nasser Al-Khelaifi show off matching suits and smiles as they confirm his move from Barcelona to Paris in 2017.

NEYMAR JR

mar's career is not yet at its peak, he still is only 25, but he
ady has set many records. There will be many more to come.

Neymar holds the record for the fastest goal in Olympic Games history. The forward struck after just 14 seconds of Brazil's match with Honduras in the semi-finals of the 2016 Rio Games, intercepting defender Johnny Palacios' pass before firing the ball home. The hosts went on to win the game 6–0.

Neymar holds the record for being the most liked Brazilian footballer in history on social media. The forward has almost 100 million likes across Facebook and Twitter, more than greats such as Kaká and Ronaldinho.

Neymar won the South American Footballer of the Year award by the biggest margin ever. The award is given to the best football player in South America by Uruguayan newspaper *El País* after voting by journalists across the continent. In 2011 Neymar won the prize, beating runner-up Eduardo Vargas by 50 points.

Although he has yet to win either award outright, Neymar is one of only two players to be the season's top goalscorer in both the Copa Libertadores and UEFA Champions League. Fellow Brazilian Mario Jardel (Gremio and Porto) is the other.

Neymar became the first Brazilian to win the Puskás Award in 2011. The then 19-year-old won the prize, which is given to the player who scores the best goal during a calendar year, for his strike against Flamengo.

Despite the initial fee reportedly being around £50 million, it was revealed in 2014 that Barcelona actually paid €88.2 million (£58.5m) to sign Neymar from Santos. At the time it was football's third highest transfer ever and is still the biggest involving a South American club.

Along with his then Barcelona teammates Lionel Messi and Luis Suárez, Neymar holds the record for the most goals by an attacking trio. The forward line scored a staggering 131 goals during the 2015–16 season, beating their previous record of 122. Before that the best effort was 100 by Messi, Samuel Eto'o and Thierry Henry in the Barça's 2008–09 treble-winning season.

Neymar broke the record for the most expensive transfer in football history when he joined Paris Saint-Germain from Barcelona for €222m (£200m) in August 2017. The deal more than doubled the previous record, set in 2016, when Manchester United paid Juventus €105m (£89m) for Paul Pogba.

THE RIO OLYMPICS

Neymar saved the 2016 Rio Olympics for the hosts by captaining Brazil to winning their first-ever football gold medal.

The South American football fans were still haunted by memories of losing 7–1 to Germany in the World Cup two years before. But now, as the two proud nations faced each other again in Rio, Neymar secured victory with the winning penalty in a dramatic shoot-out victory.

It had not looked so good for Neymar and his team when they started their quest for gold on 4 August with a goalless draw against South Africa.

There were still no goals and another 0–0 scoreline when they faced outsiders Iraq in their next group match.

Now the pressure was on. Brazil had to beat Denmark to reach the last eight. Neymar failed to score, but inspired an emphatic 4–0 win.

Fellow South Americans Colombia awaited in the quarter-finals. Neymar was motoring now and the Barcelona star scored the first goal in a 2–0 victory.

The world-famous Maracanã stadium was packed to capacity for the semi-final against Honduras on a baking hot Wednesday afternoon. Neymar, proudly wearing the iconic No.10 shirt, was again the star as he scored in the first and last minutes in a stunning 6–0 triumph.

Any celebrations were put on hold as it emerged they would have to face old rivals Germany in the final. Germany had progressed in similar fashion to Brazil, starting slowly before beating Fiji 10–0 in their final group tie and then beating Portugal and Nigeria.

Jamaican sprinter Usain Bolt was in the captivated crowd for the final as Neymar won a 26th-minute free-kick. He then stepped up to curl a brilliant shot beyond keeper Timo Horn to open the scoring.

But just as Neymar threatened to score again, opposing skipper Max Meyer silenced the stadium by equalizing to send the final into extra time and then penalties.

After seven successful spot-kicks, Weverton saved from Germany's Nils Petersen.

A nation held its breath as all eyes focused on Neymar. His time had come. And he did not disappoint as he scored in style and burst into tears of joy and relief before being mobbed by his teammates. A truly golden moment.

Neymar's penalty helped Brazil defeat Honduras in their Olympic semi-final in spectacular style. The final score was 6–0.

Neymar's celebration pays tribute to fellow Olympic gold medallist, Jamaican sprinter and big football fan Usain Bolt.

Neymar, and his victorious compatriots, check the quality of their Olympic gold medals after beating Germany in the final.

WHAT NEXT FOR NEYMAR?

When will Neymar emulate Kaká (Brazil's last winner, in 2007) and collect the FIFA Ballon d'Or as World Footballer of the Year?

Ever since he began to make waves as a teenager in the Santos youth set-up, Neymar has been compared to Pelé – the player he describes as "The King".

And, having won everything at club level by the age of 24, the rest of Neymar's career will be about joining the likes of Pelé, Diego Maradona and Johan Cruyff in the pantheon of all-time greats. It just so happens that his peers include both Lionel Messi and Cristiano Ronaldo, two others hoping to be remembered as among the best ever. They are both entering the final stages of their careers meaning soon, Neymar will stand alone as the generation's icon.

Personally, his ambition will be to add a World Cup winner's medal to his vast collection of baubles, especially considering the painful end to his 2014 campaign, when a broken vertebra ended his involvement. Given his age, he still has much time to accomplish that goal.

When he netted against Japan in a November 2017 friendly it took him to a staggering 53 goals in 83 games for his country. Given his relative youth, Pelé's all-time record of 77 Brazil goals is well within his sights. He continues to close in on Cafu's all-time appearance record of 142, with a number of major tournaments still to come before any thoughts of retirement.

At club level, his name has already been etched into folklore after Paris Saint-Germain paid by far and away football's biggest ever transfer fee. He has now made a huge impact in both Spain, with Barcelona, and France, with PSG, but after that, who knows? One thing that is for sure is that Neymar's talents could flourish in any of the world's major leagues.

Neymar has been compared to the world's greatest player ever since he made his Santos debut, and he shares a hug with the great man himself, Pelé.

Neymar wasted no time in striking up a great relationship with fellow new arrival at PSG, the brilliant young French forward Kylian Mbappé (right).

Neymar's greatest ambition is to lift the World Cup, just as former Brazil captain and the country's most-capped player, Cafu. His caps total of 142 is another Neymar target.

Even after his move to PSG, there has been speculation linking him with the leading lights in England's Premier League, while a shock return to Spain with Real Madrid has also been regularly suggested in the media. But, as ever, Neymar is focusing only on playing the game he loves.

"I'm 69 kilos," he said in August 2017. "I don't have a burden on my back. There is no pressure when you are making a dream come true.

"I try to be a good role model for my son, my family, my friends, and then I try to be a good role model for the rest of the people too."

QUIZ TIME

Here are 20 questions to test just how much you know about Neymar and his exploits for club and country.

1 How old was Neymar when he made his Santos debut?
2 Where did Neymar come in the 2015 Ballon d'Or awards?
3 How old was Neymar when he made his Brazil debut?
4 And who was the manager?
5 At which Olympics did Neymar captain his country to the gold medal?

6 What was the name of the youth side that Neymar joined in 2003?
7 In what year did Neymar first join Santos?
8 Against which club did Neymar score his first Santos goal?
9 How many goals did Neymar score in his first season at Santos?
10 Against which club did Neymar make his league debut for Paris Saint-Germain?

11 Who were the opponents when Neymar scored the goal which claimed the 2011 Puskás Award?
12 How many goals did Neymar score when PSG beat Dijon 8–0 in January 2018?
13 At what ground did Neymar scored his first Barcelona goal?
14 What was the score in Neymar's first appearance in El Clasico?
15 What number did Neymar wear when he made his Brazil debut against the USA?
16 Against which nation did Neymar make his World Cup debut?
17 In which city did Neymar make his first Champions League appearance for PSG?
18 What is the name of Neymar's son?
19 What is the name of his sister?
20 In Euros, what was the record-breaking fee which PSG paid to sign Neymar from Barcelona?